$14.95

jB   Gutman, Bill.

HARDAWAY   Anfernee

Hardaway : super

6.7-1.0

AR   shelf separate

ANFERNEE HARDAWAY

SUPER GUARD

BY BILL GUTMAN

MILLBROOK SPORTS WORLD
THE MILLBROOK PRESS
BROOKFIELD, CONNECTICUT

jB
HARDAWAY

Photographs courtesy of NBA Photos: cover (Fernando Medina), cover inset (Fernando Medina), pp. 22 (Andrew D. Bernstein), 27 (Nathaniel S. Butler), 35 (Andrew D. Bernstein), 40-41 (Nathaniel S. Butler); Focus on Sports: pp. 3, 44, 46; Allsport: pp. 4, 14 (Earl Richardson), 16, 32, 37 (Jonathan Daniel), 38, 42 (Jonathan Daniel); Memphis Commercial Appeal: pp. 9, 19; AP/Wide World Photos: pp. 11, 24, 25, 26, 31, 34; Photofest: p. 29.

Library of Congress Cataloging-in-Publication Data
Gutman, Bill.
Anfernee Hardaway : super guard / by Bill Gutman.
p. cm.
Includes index.
Summary: Examines the life of basketball player Penny Hardaway, from his childhood in Tennessee through his college days at Memphis State University to his professional career with the Orlando Magic.
ISBN 0-7613-0062-7 (lib. bdg.)
1. Hardaway, Anfernee—Juvenile literature. 2. Basketball players—United States—Biography—Juvenile literature. [1. Hardaway, Anfernee. 2. Basketball players. 3. Afro-Americans—Biography.] I. Title. II. Series.
GV884.H24G88 1997
796.323'092—dc20 [B] 96-41074 CIP AC

Published by The Millbrook Press, Inc.
2 Old New Milford Road
Brookfield, Connecticut 06804

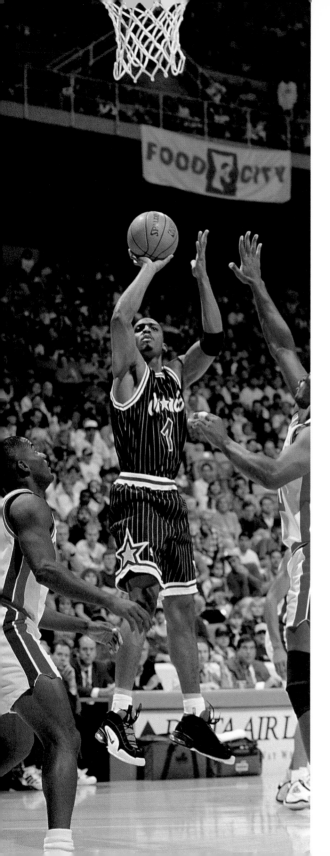

ANFERNEE HARDAWAY

The night before Thanksgiving in 1995, the Orlando Magic were playing host to the Vancouver Grizzlies at the Orlando Arena in Florida. At first glance, it seemed like an easy game for the Magic. After all, they had reached the NBA finals a year earlier and were one of the best teams in the league. The Grizzlies, on the other hand, were brand new—an expansion team beginning their first season in the NBA.

But the Magic were playing without their All-Star center, Shaquille O'Neal. Shaq had been injured in the preseason. And on this night most of the other Magic stars seemed lackluster and off their game. The Grizzlies had a real shot to win.

One player who refused to let the game get away was the Magic point guard. Anfernee "Penny" Hardaway was outstanding all night, keeping his team in the fray with his fine all-around play—scoring, passing, rebounding, and running the

When Penny gets hot, he's almost unstoppable. He has had many big games, like this one against the Milwaukee Bucks. It came just a short time after a game in which he had burned the Vancouver Grizzlies for 37 points.

offense. Yet with just 5.4 seconds left in the game, it was tied 93–93. Orlando had the ball and called a time-out.

Almost every person in the "O-rena" knew what was coming. Penny Hardaway would get the ball and take the last shot. The Grizzlies knew it, too. Sure enough, the ball came in to Hardaway at halfcourt. He dribbled toward the hoop, watching the clock carefully.

Both Vancouver guards, Greg Anthony and Byron Scott, converged on the Orlando star. With two seconds left, Hardaway suddenly made a quick move and slipped his 6-foot 7-inch (200-centimeter) frame between the two defenders. The surprised defenders were suddenly helpless, a step behind the man with the ball. They chased him, but knew they wouldn't make it.

With less than a second remaining and still about 6 feet (1.8 meters) from the hoop, Hardaway went up in the air and launched a one-handed push shot. The ball hit the front of the rim gently, bounced to the back, then returned to the front. As the buzzer sounded, it fell through the net for the winning shot. Orlando had a 95–93 victory.

What Penny Hardaway did that night was pick it up for everyone. He scored 37 of his team's 95 points to almost single-handedly win the game. But those who knew him were getting used to that kind of play. Veteran center Jon Koncak, who was playing with the Magic for the first time, summed up everyone's feelings.

"What you don't get from being on the other team is Penny's heart and soul," Koncak said. "You need a rebound? Penny gets a rebound. You need a steal? Penny gets a steal. You need a game-winning basket? Penny gets that."

Others were calling him the best all-around player in basketball. Yet at the age of 24, he was just beginning his third season in the league.

PRETTY AS A PENNY

No one can predict which child will grow up to become a great athlete. Perhaps the chances are better if the mother or father is a sports star. But no one can program athletic greatness. With many inner-city kids, staying out of trouble and getting an education are often the greatest victory of all.

For a while, it looked as if Anfernee Deon Hardaway would be one of those kids who would have to struggle just to make it through his early years. Anfernee was born in Memphis, Tennessee, on July 18, 1971. But it wasn't a good start. His father left home early and played no role in raising his only child. His mother, Fae Patterson, took care of Anfernee for his first few years.

But Fae Patterson also wanted more than just a life of poverty in Memphis. When Anfernee was in the first grade, she decided to travel to California to pursue a singing career. She couldn't take a small boy with her. That's when Anfernee had his first stroke of good luck. His grandmother, Louise Hardaway, volunteered to take him into her home.

"It was hard at first, because I felt like no one really wanted me," Anfernee said in later years. "But my grandmother proved that she loved me and cared about what happened to me."

Had it not been for her, Anfernee might have become just another lost youngster, running the streets and eventually getting into trouble. The fact that someone cared at a critical time might have actually saved his life. And that caring would later enable him to develop his superior talent as a basketball player.

"She [my grandmother] taught me simple things," Anfernee has said. "Things like keeping your word, treating people the way you want to be treated. Traditional things that have stayed with me."

But even after he moved in with his grandmother, life wasn't easy. They were very poor, living in the kind of tiny, narrow structure that was sometimes called a "shotgun" house. That's because it had just three rooms lined up one behind another. But young Anfernee appreciated it. He still does, looking back.

"It was a palace compared to the other houses I had lived in," he has said.

When his mother did return sometime later, Anfernee continued to live with his grandmother, although he remained on good terms with his mother.

Besides a lot of love, Anfernee got discipline from his grandmother. She wouldn't let him get out of line, and kept close tabs on him and the friends he had. She made sure he went to school every day and took him to church on Sundays.

Anfernee was always very thin, almost frail, as a youth, and Louise Hardaway didn't want anything to happen to him. In fact, it was his tiny, innocent face that led Louise Hardaway to give her grandson the nickname that has stayed with him to this day.

"He's pretty as a penny," she once said.

And after that, Anfernee was always known as "Penny" Hardaway.

BASKETBALL AND THE BOOKS

Like many youngsters, Penny soon began playing sports. He grew taller but remained thin. It wasn't long before basketball became his favorite activity. His build was best suited to the court game, and his skills began to improve. His grandmother continued to be strict with him, making sure he went to school every day and kept up with his schoolwork.

As Penny grew taller, he began to feel that basketball was a way for him to stand out, to get approval from others. And by the time he arrived at Treadwell High School in the fall of 1987, he was well on his way to becoming a fine, all-around player. He was already well over 6 feet (183 centimeters) tall and still growing.

Though he remained thin, his talent enabled him to match up against stronger players. And once he began playing for Treadwell, it began to look as if Penny was a star in the making.

For the first time in his life, he was the center of attention. People looked up to him as a school hero, a real star. Soon Penny began to dream of being a star in college and then going on to become an NBA player with all the money that comes with it.

By the start of his senior season of 1989–1990, he had become so good that college recruiters were starting to come in droves just to watch him perform. He had developed into a player who could do everything on the court. Though he was already at his full height of 6 feet 7 inches (200 centimeters), he could handle the ball better than anyone on the team.

He could also shoot, rebound, pass, play excellent defense, and block shots. He began to pile up numbers that ranked him with

It was at Treadwell High School in Memphis that Penny first became a real star. As a senior, he averaged 36.6 points per game.

any high school player in the country. Garmer Currie, Jr., said that he was a quiet kid who was easy to coach. But even then, Penny let certain things bother him.

"Penny always kept pretty much to himself and never bragged or flaunted his great skills," the coach said. "But even then he always worried about what people or the media might say about him. He could handle the pressure of a tight game, but often had difficulty handling criticism."

When the season ended, Penny led the entire state with a 36.6 scoring average. That's incredible when you realize that a high school game is just 32 minutes long. He was scoring more than a point a minute.

Yet even with his tremendous scoring touch, Penny still found time to grab 10.1 rebounds a game, pass for 6.2 assists, make 3.3 steals, and block 2.8 shots in every contest. He was not only named Mr. Basketball in the state of Tennessee but was also chosen *Parade* magazine's National High School Player of the Year.

His only disappointment was that Treadwell had never won a state title. Yet it seemed that he would have his pick of nearly any college he wanted, all over the country.

But between the end of the basketball season and the end of the school year, Penny began having problems in school. Being a basketball star and not paying enough attention to his studies had finally taken a toll. He failed an algebra course. Then he did very poorly the first time he took his college board exams. Suddenly, one of the best high school basketball players in the country found himself being called too dumb to go college.

Once again, Penny realized how fast things can go bad. And once again his grandmother stepped in to help. She pushed him to study harder. She also worked with him at home and kept his spirits up when things looked bleak. He took the college boards again. This time he did well enough to be accepted into school, but not well enough to be eligible to play ball his freshman year.

In July of 1990, Penny played in the Olympic Festival, a tournament for top high school players held in Minneapolis. Here he makes a move on Damon Bailey, who would go on to star at Indiana.

Now the question was where to go. Penny could easily have gone to one of the so-called basketball glamour schools. These schools are always in the top 10 and have a chance for the national championship. He was surely good enough to play for any of them. But he surprised a lot of people when he decided to stay close to home.

In the fall of 1990, Penny enrolled at Memphis State University (now called the University of Memphis). In effect, he was staying in a city where he already had a reputation, where people already knew and respected his talents. And by going to Memphis State, he was sending a message that he loved the city enough to stay there. And Memphis loved him for that.

A NEAR TRAGEDY

After making his decision, Penny knew he would have a difficult freshman year. He couldn't play in 1990–1991 because the NCAA's academic rules said that he had to prove himself as a student first. For a competitive athlete, not playing his sport is almost torture. A person of lesser character might not have gone to college at all. But because of the values he received from his grandmother, Penny wasn't about to quit.

So he watched as the Tigers had a 17–15 season and went to the postseason National Invitational Tournament. Larry Finch was the Memphis State coach. He was a former All-American guard for the Tigers and had been the coach since 1986–1987. During that time the Tigers had never had a losing season. Now Coach Finch hoped that he would have Penny available for 1991.

Instead of trying to slide through, Penny worked hard at his studies. He quickly proved that he could be a capable student. His grades were fine, and he was cleared to play as a sophomore in 1991. The school had also signed 6-foot 9-inch (206-centimeter) David Vaughn, another high school All-American. The team looked like it would be very strong.

In 1991–1992, the Tigers left the Metro Conference after 16 seasons and joined the newly formed Great Midwest Conference. They also began to play in a new arena, the Pyramid. It was one of the largest Division 1-A facilities in the country, seating 20,142 people for basketball. Penny was in an exciting situation.

But it almost hadn't happened. In fact, Penny could have seen his basketball career and perhaps even his life ended on a Memphis street in April 1991. Penny and a friend were walking at night when a man with a gun jumped out of a car and demanded their money.

Penny and his friend didn't resist. The gunman took what money they had and told them to lie down on the sidewalk. He then jumped back into the car, which was driven by another man. As the car sped away, the gunman fired several shots from the moving car. Maybe it was just a warning for the boys not to try to get the license plate or to follow. But one of the bullets bounced off the pavement and slammed into Penny's right foot.

The force of the bullet broke three small metatarsal bones in the foot. Fortunately, the bones weren't shattered, and the foot was placed in a cast that went all the way up to Penny's knee. The bullet, however, remained lodged in his foot, in an area the doctors felt was too difficult to operate on. But Penny was very lucky. The doctors predicted that he would be fine.

BACK ON THE COURT

By the time basketball practice started on October 15, Penny was ready. He practiced for 11 days with the bullet still in his foot. All the running and jumping finally caused the bullet to move to a better spot in his foot, and on October 26 it was removed. Penny recovered completely.

When Penny joined the team, he was still rusty from his layoff and the foot injury. Yet Coach Finch could see right away that Penny had all the tools to be a standout. He was a player who could do everything well on the basketball court. There was no doubt that he would be a starter.

Penny officially started at forward for the Tigers. But it was soon apparent that he would be handling the ball. Almost from the start, the ball would be in Penny's hands in crucial situations. Yet on defense he often guarded the other

After being shot in the foot during a street robbery in Memphis in April of 1991, Penny recovered to start his first college season for Memphis State that fall.

team's best forward and sometimes even its center. Only a special kind of player can do this well.

He began making his mark early. After the Tigers lost two of their first three games, Penny exploded for 31 points with 7 rebounds and 4 steals in a 105–97 win over Southwest Louisiana. Two games later, he handed out 12 assists as Memphis State whipped Jackson State, 87–73. Despite missing a year of play, Penny Hardaway had returned with all the skills and excitement he had demonstrated before, and more.

For the remainder of the season, Penny established himself as one of the most exciting young college players in the land. He led the Tigers in scoring and in many other statistical categories. After an 8–6 first half, the Tigers finished the second half of the regular season by winning 10 of their final 13 games.

The team had a big 92–88 win over fifth-ranked Arkansas and a 68–67 victory over 21st-ranked Tulane. Once the regular season ended, the Tigers topped DePaul before losing to Cincinnati in the Great Midwest

Conference tournament. The team then received a bid to the Midwest Region of the NCAA tournament.

In their first tournament game, Penny scored 21 points and led the club with 8 rebounds as the Tigers topped Pepperdine, 80–70. In the second round they upset Arkansas again, this time by 82–80, as David Vaughn hit the game-winner with five seconds left. Vaughn had 26, while Penny had 14.

Next came the Regional semifinals at Kansas City. The Tigers met Georgia Tech in an exciting game in which they came back in the final seconds to force an overtime. In OT, Memphis State hit 9 of 10 free throws to help them to an 83–79 victory. Penny again was outstanding, scoring a team-leading 24 points. Now the club was one win away from a trip to the Final Four.

But then they ran into an old nemesis. Cincinnati beat the Tigers for the fourth time in the season, this time by a lopsided 88–57 count. Penny still led his team, but with just 12 points. The Tigers' season was over.

But in his first college season, Anfernee Hardaway had averaged 17.4 points and 7.0 rebounds per game. He also had 188 assists, 86 steals, and 45 blocks. His postseason honors included being named the Most Valuable Player in the Great Midwest Conference and an Associated Press honorable mention All-American.

He had done everything asked of him, but the best was yet to come.

FIRST TEAM ALL-AMERICAN

Returning for his junior season of 1992–1993, Penny was touted as a possible All-American. Though he weighed less than 200 pounds (90 kilograms), he was wire-hard and in top shape. He had a year under his belt, and that summer he was one of eight collegiate stars picked to train with the 1992 Olympic Dream Team.

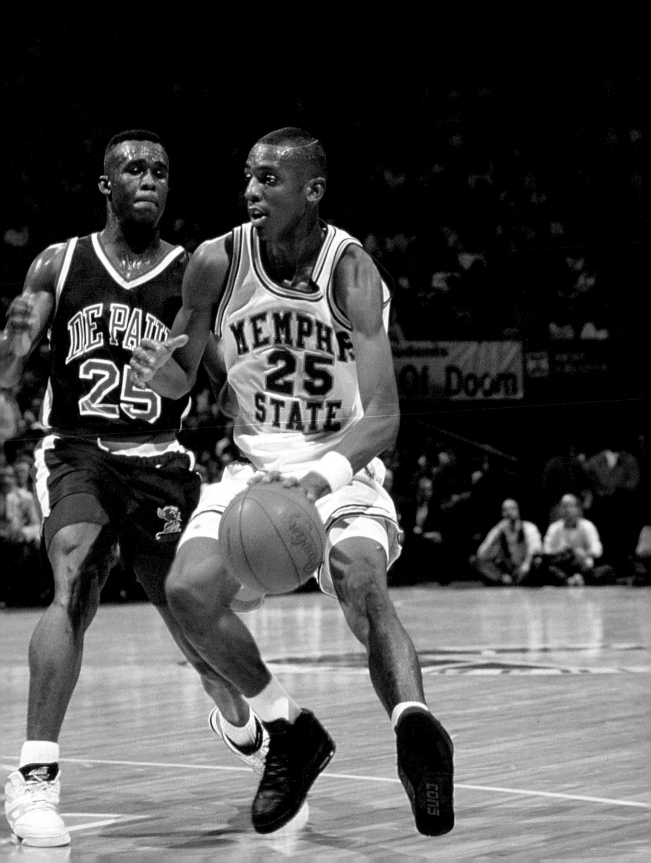

The Dream Team was made up of NBA superstars, and training with them gave Penny even more confidence when the Tigers' season started. This time it didn't take long for Penny Hardaway to show the basketball world that he was not only one of the best but also one of the most electrifying players anywhere.

Though the Tigers lost to Arkansas in their opener, 81–76, Penny opened a lot of eyes. In that game, he connected on six three-point shots from long range. And his fine, all-around floor play kept his team close. Unfortunately, the Tigers lost sophomore star David Vaughn to a season-ending injury in that game. That would hurt.

But with Penny Hardaway in the lineup, the Tigers had the ability to beat any team. Against Chaminade, Penny had 33 points, including seven three-pointers. In the next game, an overtime win over Brigham Young, he scored a career-high 37 with six more three-pointers dropping through the net. He was also doing the job on defense and handing out assists to his teammates.

As the Memphis basketball media guide said, "Hardaway also had the ability to make at least one play every game that would leave an entire crowd, at home or on the road, shaking their heads in total amazement. He was truly a special player."

Not only were the fans marveling at Penny's electrifying game, but the pros were looking, too. NBA scouts already were touting Penny as a future top draft choice. When his coach was asked to pick Penny's most breathtaking play, he was stumped.

As a junior in 1992–1993, Penny led the Tigers to the NCAA Tournament. His great all-around game also made him a First Team All-American.

"Picking a favorite Penny Hardaway play is like picking out which one of the stars up in the sky shines the brightest," said Larry Finch. "There's so many of 'em, you can't just pick one."

As for Penny, he admitted that he enjoyed entertaining the crowds with his great talent.

"I like to entertain," he said. "Most of all, I want to win. But when I do something special, I can feel the vibe from the crowd. I live for the *ooh*, the *aah*."

Against Georgia State in the 11th game of the season, Penny had 21 points, 15 rebounds, and 14 assists as the Tigers won, 97–76. It was the first triple-double (double digits in three statistical categories) in Memphis State history. In the next game, against 18th-ranked Vanderbilt, he did it again. This time he scored 26 points, took down 12 rebounds, and passed for 10 assists as the Tigers won again, 84–78.

His great play continued. Though he was quiet and often kept to himself, he had become the most popular athlete in Memphis. Coach Finch said it was because he had stayed home to play ball.

"The people here just about worship him. He could have gone to college anywhere, but he stayed right here. He knew nobody was going to love him the way they loved him right in his own backyard."

The Tigers finished the regular season at 19–10, then beat St. Louis in the first round of the Great Midwest Conference tournament before losing to Cincinnati, 77–72. The team still received a bid to the Southeast Region of the NCAA tournament. But there they lost to a good Western Kentucky team, 55–52, ending their season.

Despite the final loss, Penny had put together an incredible season. He set a school record with 729 points, good for a 22.8 average. He also led the team

*Penny's grandmother (left) and mother share a proud moment as Penny is honored
at Memphis State. At right is his coach, Larry Finch.*

in rebounding with 8.5 a game, assists (6.4), and steals. He was the Great Midwest Conference Player of the Year, and a finalist for all the major Player of the
Year awards. In addition, he was named to almost every first-team All-America
squad. But perhaps the greatest compliment of all came from the legendary
Earvin "Magic" Johnson.

After watching Penny play several times, Magic Johnson said, "He reminds
me of. . .me."

TURNING PRO

Penny had now been at Memphis State for three years. He was an education major and had worked hard at his studies. In fact, he had a 3.4 cumulative grade-point average. There was little doubt that in another year he would graduate with his class.

But he also had a big decision to make. In the eyes of most, he was already an accomplished basketball player who was ready to go to the NBA. If he left school before his senior year and entered the NBA draft, he was a likely lottery pick, probably one of the top three candidates. And top picks were getting huge, multimillion-dollar contracts.

Penny had to weigh all these things. If he came out now, he would finally be able to take care of his family. They had lived in poverty so long. Another year at Memphis could be a risk. What if he suffered a serious injury that ended or slowed his pro career? He spoke with his family, friends, and advisers, and decided to enter the 1993 NBA draft.

The team with the first choice in that draft was the Orlando Magic. A year earlier the Magic, an expansion team that had begun play in 1989–1990, had taken 7-foot 1-inch (238-centimeter) center Shaquille O'Neal. O'Neal was Rookie of the Year and was expected to become one of the great centers in NBA history. With Shaq in the lineup, the Magic had improved from 21–61 the year before to 41–41, a .500 record. They had missed the playoffs by one game and then lucked out in the draft lottery to get the top pick.

Most people felt that the Magic would use their top pick to take Chris Webber, a 6-foot 10-inch (208-centimeter) power forward from Michigan. The feeling was that if Webber teamed with O'Neal on the front line, the team would be able to overpower anyone. Philadelphia had the second pick and indicated that it would choose a thin, 7-foot 6-inch (229-centimeter) center named Shawn

Bradley. The Golden State Warriors picked third, and that was the team rumored to want Penny.

But Penny had other ideas. He had met Shaquille O'Neal before, and the two had become friends. He felt that if he could team with a young center like Shaq, the two of them could really make a mark in the NBA. But he had to convince the Magic that he would serve the team better than Webber.

New players are allowed to work out for teams before the draft. Webber's predraft workout with the Magic was a media event. Many reporters and photographers were there. But Penny's wasn't so spectacular. He had to bum a ride into town with a single cameraman and had his breakfast at a fast-food restaurant. The workout didn't seem to change things in the Orlando camp. General Manager Pat Williams was still leaning toward Webber.

Penny, however, wouldn't quit. He sent the Magic a life-size cardboard poster of himself so they wouldn't forget him. Then he called Williams and asked for a second workout. They granted it the night before the draft, and this time Penny really showed his stuff.

"I've never seen someone come in and do things that Penny Hardaway did in that workout," said Williams. "He was making passes and dunks that would have had crowds screaming in disbelief if they had been there. Never before, that I know of, has a team had its thinking changed so dramatically 24 hours before a draft."

Knowing the Warriors would love to have Webber, Orlando and Golden State went into some heated negotiations. If the Magic simply chose Hardaway, then Philadelphia might take Webber with the second pick. That would leave the Warriors without either player. The Magic could do better by making a deal.

On draft day, the suspense built. NBA Commissioner David Stern stepped to the podium and announced that the Orlando Magic had picked Chris Webber.

Penny was the third pick in the 1993 NBA draft, taken by the Golden State Warriors. Moments later, he was traded to the Orlando Magic for Chris Webber, the number one pick. A surprised Penny (left) and Webber immediately exchanged caps.

There were about 8,000 fans gathered at the Orlando Arena to watch the draft. When the announcement was made, they cheered.

Then Philadelphia, as expected, tabbed Shawn Bradley. The Warriors were next. Commissioner Stern announced that Golden State had taken Anfernee Hardaway. But within minutes, there was another announcement. Stern returned to say that Orlando had traded the rights to Webber to Golden State in return for Hardaway and three future draft choices. It was a blockbuster trade.

At the draft site, Hardaway and Webber exchanged the team caps they had donned just minutes before. And at the Orlando Arena, the fans who had been cheering minutes before began to boo. They all felt Webber would help their team more. They really didn't know much about Penny as a player. It was Pat Williams who then grabbed a microphone at the O-rena and tried to quiet the crowd.

"Those of you who are upset, your jeers will turn to cheers," he said. "Your first look at Anfernee Hardaway will thrill your hearts."

WINNING OVER THE FANS

When Penny heard about the booing at the Orlando Arena, it hurt him. He had been sensitive to criticism before, but his home fans had always loved him. His college coach, Larry Finch, had once said that he was as popular in Memphis as another hometown legend, the late singer Elvis Presley. Now, he was being jeered just for being drafted.

He finally signed a 13-year deal worth some $65 million just before training camp began. Though he and his family would never be poor again, the fans showed their disapproval by booing him again during his first preseason game.

"How can you feel at home when your hometown fans boo you?" Anfernee asked.

GM Pat Williams felt compelled to defend the trade. "I've been in basketball a long time," Williams said, "and Penny showed me things I haven't seen. We've got a guy who will run our ballclub for the next 12 or 15 years."

The problem was that Chris Webber and his Michigan teammates had been in the NCAA finals two straight years. Webber had been on the national stage much more than Penny and Memphis State. He was viewed as a "can't miss" pro prospect. Penny still had to prove himself.

Then when the Magic lost a preseason game to Miami in which Penny didn't play well but was still picked as the game's best substitute, the fans booed again. That led assistant coach Bob Hill to hang a note on Penny's locker that said:

"Penny, ignore this type of reaction from fickle fans. They will come to love you and appreciate what you can do for this team and our community. Stay focused, work hard, and have fun. I'm always around to talk."

Penny addresses the media in Orlando after signing his first pro contract with the Magic. Many fans booed him at first because they thought Webber was a better choice. But it wouldn't be long before the jeers turned to cheers.

The boos were something new to Penny, who said, "I've been loved everywhere I've ever played." But he had played all his life in Memphis, where the fans had known him for years. In Orlando, he was starting over in a new place. In addition, he had to adjust to play in the NBA.

Early in the season, the Magic continued to use veteran Scott Skiles at point guard. Penny was the starter at shooting or two guard. But at times, when Skiles was out of the game, Penny would swing over to the point. Though just a rookie, he was seeing more court time than anyone but center O'Neal.

With Shaq up among the league leaders in scoring and rebounding, and with solid support from Skiles, Nick Anderson, Dennis Scott, and others, the Magic were winning. Add the rookie Hardaway, and the team was second to only the New York Knicks in the Atlantic Division of the Eastern Conference.

Though Penny was inconsistent early in the season, he showed flashes of greatness to come. On November 23, the Magic played host to Golden State and Chris

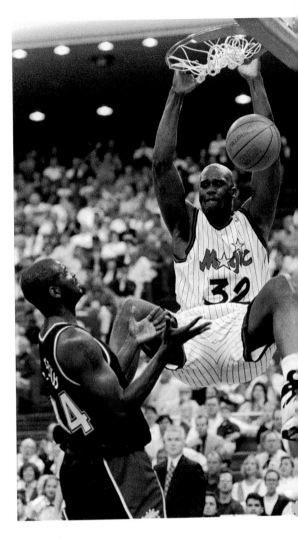

Before Penny joined the Magic, opposing teams had to deal mostly with the power game of star center Shaquille O'Neal (32). Penny gave the Magic an all-around floor game and worked with Shaq to make Orlando a top team.

Penny scored 22 points in the Rookie Game during NBA All-Star Weekend and was aptly named the game's Most Valuable Player.

Webber. Orlando won the game, 120–107. Penny scored 23 points and added 8 rebounds. Webber, by contrast, had just 13 points and 10 rebounds. Late in the game, a group of Magic fans unfurled a banner that read: We Picked the Right One, Baby, Uh Huh.

But it wasn't until the season was nearly half over that Penny began asserting himself. He was named Rookie of the Month for January 1994 when he averaged 20.5 points, 7.0 assists, 5.7 rebounds, and 3.33 steals per game. In late February, Penny played in the Rookie Game during All-Star Weekend and was named the game's Most Valuable Player. He had 22 points and 3 assists in just 22 minutes of action.

After the All-Star break, he began taking even more of a leadership role with the team. And he was also playing more at point guard. Against the Celtics on April 15, he had the first triple-double of his NBA career, scoring 14 points and adding 12 assists and 11 rebounds. Now his fine all-around game was coming to the fore.

He was again Rookie of the Month in April when he averaged 19.3 points, 8.2 assists, 6.6 rebounds, and 2.15 steals. He was doing it all. Against Golden State on March 22, he had a season-high 15 assists. He had grabbed a season-best 13 rebounds against Milwaukee in February. His numbers for a guard, and a rookie guard, were almost astonishing. Even Shaquille O'Neal began to see his teaming with Penny as something special.

"Once we get a few years under our belt," Shaq said, "Penny and I will be the Magic and Kareem of the 90s."

Shaquille was referring to point guard Magic Johnson and center Kareem Abdul-Jabbar of the L.A. Lakers, both all-time greats. The duo had led the Lakers to five NBA titles.

"That's a lot to live up to," Penny said when he heard about Shaq's statement. "But I think we have a chance to someday be worthy of that comparison. To be the best, you have to think like the best."

By the end of his rookie year, Penny had become an outstanding pro player. He could score from the outside or use his quickness and leaping ability to go underneath and hold his own against bigger, stronger players.

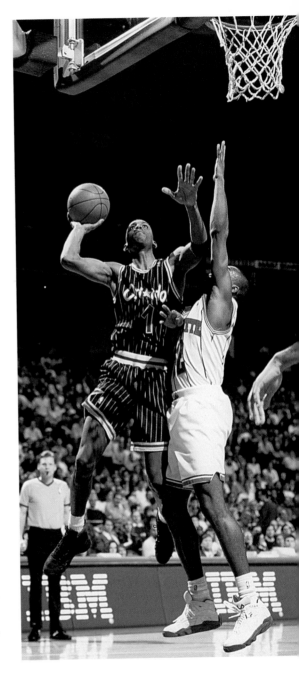

The Magic finished the 1993–1994 season with a 50–32 record, the best in franchise history, though seven games behind the division-winning Knicks. Then, in the playoffs, the inexperienced Magic were beaten by the Indiana Pacers in three straight games. Yet there was little doubt that something big was beginning in Orlando.

As for Penny, he had a sensational rookie year. He started all 82 games, averaging 16.0 points a game. He also averaged 6.6 assists, 5.4 rebounds, and set a team record with 190 steals, or 2.32 a game. After the season he was named to the NBA All-Rookie first team.

Then, in the closest voting since 1981, Penny finished second to Chris Webber for NBA Rookie of the Year. Only six votes separated the two players who had been traded for each other on draft day. Each looked as if he would be great. But Penny appeared to be in the better team situation.

NBA FIRST TEAM ALL-STAR

Prior to the 1994–1995 season, Penny had another notable experience. He and teammate Shaquille O'Neal had featured roles in a major motion picture. *Blue Chips* was about a fictitious college basketball program and the young players recruited to play there. The film starred Nick Nolte, but both Penny and Shaq had speaking parts besides showing their court talents.

Then, before rejoining the Magic, Penny once again strained his image with the fans. There was a clause in Penny's contract that gave him the right to renegotiate after his rookie year. So once again he went into a long contract negotiation with the Magic. Rumors surfaced that Penny was asking for an unheard-of amount of money.

He finally signed a new nine-year contract for about $70 million. The money was close to that of the first contract, but the term was shorter. When he joined

This is basketball, Hollywood style. After his rookie year, Penny had a featured role in the movie Blue Chips. *He played a freshman recruit at a fictitious university. Here he scores in the usual way, but he also did well as an actor.*

the team for a preseason game, he was booed again. Not knowing the nuts and bolts of contract negotiations and the changing market in the NBA, many saw Penny as just another greedy athlete. They forgot that he was an extremely talented player who gave his all every game. Once again, however, the criticism bothered him.

It continued into the season. When the Magic lost the opening game to Washington, Penny was again booed and criticized in the press.

"Here, it's yea if you hit the shot and boo if you miss," he said. "After we lost to Washington, all I heard on the radio was how the Magic needed a traditional point guard, how I wasn't the right guy to run the offense. Sometimes the fans here make me feel wanted, and sometimes they don't."

Why wasn't Penny a traditional point guard? The answer was simple. He did so much more on the court than most point guards. And at the beginning of his second season, many people still didn't know how good he could be. But they were about to find out.

On December 2 against the New York Knicks, Penny took the ball to the hoop and dunked over the Knicks' 7-foot center, Patrick Ewing. "Tree" Rollins, the Magic's backup center that year, was one of many who couldn't believe what had happened.

"Patrick is seven feet and about 250 pounds, and Penny is six-seven and skinny as a rail," Rollins said. "When Penny took off for the hoop, I thought Patrick would either get the block or flatten him. But Penny just exploded to the basket, and, *wham*! It was over."

Penny was quickly silencing his critics. He was the NBA's Player of the Week at the end of November when he averaged 32.3 points, 6.5 rebounds, 6.5 assists, and 2.5 steals a game. In a game against Milwaukee that week he had another triple-double, this time with 35 points, 12 assists, and 10 rebounds.

Magic Coach Brian Hill said the fans in Orlando were really beginning to appreciate Penny's skills.

At the start of the 1994–1995 season Penny was playing at the superstar level. Here he cuts between a pair of Atlanta defenders for another two points.

Always eager to learn and improve his game, Penny listens whenever Orlando coach Brian Hill speaks.

"I think the community has a greater affection for him than he thinks they do," the coach said. "When the player introductions start, nobody gets a louder ovation than Penny Hardaway."

The Magic had signed free-agent power forward Horace Grant during the offseason and were now considered one of the elite teams in the league. And Penny just seemed to get better and better. He was named a starter for the East in the annual All-Star Game in February. Playing with the cream of the crop, Penny scored 12 points, had a team high 11 assists, and grabbed 5 rebounds.

There was little doubt that he had become a superstar in just his second season. Yet he was still quiet off the court and liked his privacy.

"All I want people around here to know about me is that I'm a good person," he said. "I don't really want them to get to know too much about me. I'm just very private."

By the time the season ended, however, it wasn't easy for Penny to remain private. He had just put together an outstanding season, averaging 20.9 points and 7.2 assists a game. As in college, fans never knew when he would do something absolutely spectacular. The Magic won their division with a 57–25 record, and Penny was named an NBA First Team All-Star.

GOING FOR THE TOP

Entering the 1995 playoffs, it looked as if the Magic would have a good chance to win the championship. And it couldn't come soon enough for Penny. He had seen so many things go wrong in his life that he never counted too much on tomorrow.

"I really want to win everything this year," he said. "You never know what's going to happen. We could have injuries. There could be trades. This might be our only time we ever have to compete for it all."

For a while it looked as if the Magic might do it. In the first round they topped the Boston Celtics in four games. Next they had to play the Chicago Bulls. The Bulls were given a good chance since their star Michael Jordan had rejoined the team a few weeks before the end of the regular season, ending a brief retirement.

But the young Magic prevailed in six games as Jordan showed that he was still rusty. At the same time, Penny showed that he could be the next all-around star in the league. In the sixth and final game, which the Magic won, 108–102, Penny had an incredible first half, scoring 19 points. And he did it in a head-to-head matchup with Jordan.

"Jordan started the game matched up against Hardaway and was taken to school early and often by Orlando's All-Star point guard," said one newspaper. "Hardaway produced 19 first half points and hit four three-pointers, including a trey with 19 seconds remaining in the second quarter."

Now the Magic went up against the Indiana Pacers for the Eastern Conference title and a chance to go to the finals. This one went the full seven games, with the Magic winning the finale, 105–81. Penny had just 17 points in that seventh game, but he had impressed everyone, including Indiana's veteran coach, Larry Brown.

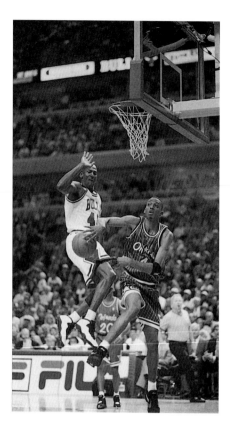

In a 1995 playoff game against Michael Jordan and the Chicago Bulls, Penny was brilliant. Here he throws a no-look pass behind him as Jordan leaps into the air looking to block a shot that never came.

"Watching Penny Hardaway play is like gazing into a crystal ball, like watching the game evolve before your very eyes," Brown said. "Maybe someday it won't be so rare to see players with as wide a range of skills as he has. I just hope I'm around to see it."

Now Penny and the Magic were in the finals. They would have to face the defending champion Houston Rockets. The Rockets were led by two veteran superstars, center Hakeem Olajuwon and guard Clyde Drexler. Once again Penny told everyone how badly he wanted to win.

"I can remember the agony I had from high school and college, not winning those big games we were in," he said. "Now having the chance we do right now, I probably won't get in this situation again, so I have to take advantage of it."

Penny and his teammates tried hard. But Olajuwon and Drexler both played incredible basketball, and the Rockets won the first three games. A four-game sweep was almost unthinkable to Penny, Shaq, and the other Magic players.

"We're not thinking like that [being swept], not thinking of being down 3–0,"

Penny said. "We're only thinking of getting this down to a one-game series, and getting it back to Orlando, our court."

There was no quit in the Magic, but this time the Rockets were just too good. Houston won game four to take its second-straight championship. The young Orlando team was beaten, but most experts felt that they would be back. With both Penny and Shaq just 24 years old, there was little doubt that the team would stay close to the top.

Penny had played well against the Rockets, averaging 25.5 points in the four games and leading both

Off the court, Penny is a private person who likes to hang with old friends he can trust. Few people would know he is one of the best basketball players in the world.

clubs with 32 assists. But the bottom line is winning, and the Magic didn't do it. Yet there was no doubt that Penny's star was still on the rise.

"I wish I had his height, I wish I had his speed, I wish I had his vision," said Detroit's Joe Dumars, himself an all-star guard. "But most of all, I wish I had his future."

Penny was still a very private person. He lived in Orlando with two old friends, people he could trust. His best friend on the Magic was veteran guard Brian Shaw, who acknowledged that Penny was "always dealing with outsiders who want to uncover something about him."

But Penny knew he had to learn to deal with everything that went with being a superstar athlete.

"I guess if there was one thing I need to work on it is taking criticism," he said. "I'm getting better at it. I just had a hard time understanding it when I was younger. Having your whole life under a microscope changes you, you know."

That was true. And Penny was still getting better at basketball. He returned for the 1995–1996 season some 15 pounds (7 kilograms) heavier, the result of an offseason of weight training. He now weighed nearly 215 pounds (98 kilograms), and he could no longer be described as scrawny.

He was also becoming more public. He had signed a shoe contract with Nike that led to a popular television commercial in which Penny trades quips with a wise-cracking puppet likeness of himself called Little Penny. He seemed natural and relaxed in the TV spot, just as he had when he filmed *Blue Chips*. He was also chosen as a member of Dream Team II, which represented the United States at the 1996 Olympic Games in Atlanta, Georgia, and won the gold medal in basketball.

Becoming more involved in the community, he also set up "Penny's Pals," a pledge program for corporations and individuals designed to raise money for four local charities. Those participating in the program pledged a donation for every slam dunk made by Penny during the 1995–1996 season. He is also an important member of the Campaign for Community Values. With this organization, Penny and others speak on behalf of curbing violence in Orange County, where Orlando is located.

In the 1995–1996 preseason, the Magic suffered a setback. Shaquille O'Neal sustained a broken thumb that caused him to miss the first few weeks of the season. The starting center was veteran Jon Koncak, and most people felt that the team would be lucky to win half its games without the big guy in the middle.

What no one counted on was the incredible play of Anfernee Hardaway. Penny simply took over the team and made sure that the Magic kept winning, even without Shaq. In the opener against Cleveland, Penny had 28 points and 8 assists. In game three against Washington he hit for 25 points and added 10 assists. On the next night, against New Jersey, he had a career-high 42 points and 8 more assists.

After six games Penny was averaging 27.2 points, 6.2 rebounds, and 7.3 assists. The team lost only once as Penny was named NBA Player of the Week.

"Penny took all the offensive burden on himself," said Coach Hill, "while still directing the team from the point guard spot. It was probably the finest stretch of games I've seen Penny play."

With Shaquille O'Neal injured at the start of the 1995–1996 season, Penny took charge of the team and was sensational. Here he dunks over Bulls center Luc Longley.

Everyone respects Penny's game now, including the great Magic Johnson, who once said Penny reminded him of himself. Here Magic greets Penny warmly before the start of a game.

Then on November 14, against Michael Jordan and the Chicago Bulls, Penny shone more brightly than ever. The game was close all the way. Penny had to work hard on both offense and defense. He was hitting on both jumpers and drives. Then, with just over a minute left, Penny calmly drained a clutch three-pointer. This, with four free throws by Nick Anderson, closed out a 94–88 Orlando win.

For the game, Penny had hit on 12 of 18 shots from the field, scoring 36 points. He also had 4 rebounds, 5 steals, and a bushel of assists. It was an all-around effort and earned Penny even more praise.

"For Penny to outplay both of those guys [Jordan and Scottie Pippen], that was just something to watch," said Magic center Jon Koncak. "Right now, Penny's as good as it gets."

Peter Vecsey, a longtime basketball writer who had seen decades of great players, said he couldn't think of another player whose long jump shots were so athletic looking. Then he added how Penny's footwork and ability to get off the jump shot were so different from those of most players.

"He can be fast-breaking with an opponent riding his hip and, without warning, root and shoot. Nothing anybody can do about it, either," wrote Vecsey. "And this is only his third season."

Penny continued to play like a demon. The team compiled a 17–5 record before Shaquille O'Neal returned. Once the big guy was back, Orlando continued to be one of the elite teams in the league. The Magic finished the regular season with a 60–22 record, winning another Atlantic Division title. It was also the third-best record in the league.

As for Penny, he was once again an NBA First Team All-Star, having played in all 82 games. He averaged 21.7 points, 11th best in the league, and had 7.1 assists, and 2.02 steals per contest. But the real goal for Penny and his teammates was the NBA championship.

The club marched through the early rounds of the playoffs. First they swept the Detroit Pistons in three straight. In the Conference semifinals they whipped the Atlanta Hawks in five games, 4–1. Next, however, they had to play the record-setting Chicago Bulls, a team that had an amazing 72–10 regular-season record.

Chicago had the great Michael Jordan, Scottie Pippen, and Dennis Rodman to lead them and were determined to make up for their loss to the Magic the season before. This time they made it look almost easy. They won the first game, 121–83. Only Penny kept the Magic in it, scoring 38 points. The team also lost Horace Grant to an elbow injury.

The series ended in an embarrassing four-game sweep. Jordan had 45 points in the fourth and final game. That sent the Magic home with a bad feeling in their stomachs.

"Getting swept is just a sickening feeling," Penny said. "It's even worse because we are a better team than we displayed. Even with the injuries, it's still hard to take that and live with it."

Penny averaged 23.3 points in 12 play-off games, but some critics felt that the supporting cast needed an overhaul. There were even rumors that Shaq might leave the team via free agency. None of that made Penny happy.

"I just have to play with who's here," he said. "I think there's an attitude among everyone that this group is solid and should stay together. I love this team that I'm with right now."

In the minds of many, Penny was the key to the team's eventually getting a title. That theory will be tested fully beginning in the 1996–1997 season. During the offseason, Shaquille O'Neal surprised everyone by leaving the Magic and signing with the Los Angeles Lakers. With the big guy gone, the Magic are surely now Penny's team.

When Shaq was injured early in the 1995–1996 season, Penny played the best

Penny was a first team All-Star again in 1995–1996. He can do it all on the court, like drive around fellow superstar Scottie Pippen of the Bulls.

basketball of his life, leading the Magic to a 17–5 start. Now he'll be called upon to rise to even greater challenges, since the team won't have a dominant center. Most feel the best of Penny Hardaway is still to come.

Happier in Orlando than he had ever been before, the usually reserved and cautious Hardaway has admitted, "I think they appreciate my skills in Orlando now."

But Magic vice president of basketball operations John Gabriel has made it more emphatic than that. "Everybody loves Penny now," he has said. "I don't expect that will change."

As for Penny, he continues to work on his game. He remains a private person close to only his family and a few friends. He never brags, but has a quiet confidence about his skills and his ability to help his team win. And he appreciates the things he has achieved. But no matter how great it gets, he also remembers the one person who made it possible.

"Being an All-America, a first-round draft pick in the NBA, acting in a movie, and now playing with a player as great as Shaq, those are things I never could have dreamed of growing up in a little house in Memphis with my grandmother," Penny has said. "Everything I've accomplished started with her."

Penny Hardaway, a
full-fledged NBA
superstar.

ANFERNEE HARDAWAY: HIGHLIGHTS

1971   Born on July 18 in Memphis, Tennessee.

1987   Enters Treadwell High School.

1990   Leads the entire state with a 36.6 scoring average.
Named *Parade* magazine's National High School Player
of the Year.
Named Mr. Basketball in Tennessee.
Enters Memphis State University (now the University of Memphis)
but sits out his freshman year.

1991   Starts at forward for University of Memphis Tigers in his sophomore year.

1992   Named Great Midwest Conference Most Valuable Player.

1993   During the 1992–1993 season, sets a University of Memphis scoring record
with 729 points, or 22.8 per game.
Named Great Midwest Conference Most Valuable Player for the second time.
Is selected by the Golden State Warriors in the first round (third pick overall) of
the NBA draft, but is immediately traded to the Orlando Magic for number-one
pick Chris Webber and three future draft choices.

1994   Named Most Valuable Player in the Rookie Game at All-Star Weekend.
Named to NBA All-Rookie First Team.
Is runner-up, behind Chris Webber, for NBA Rookie of the Year.
Posts his first triple-double on April 15 with 14 points, 12 assists, and 11
rebounds.
Helps lead the Orlando Magic to a 50–32 record, best in franchise history, and its
first playoff appearance.

1995   Named as a starter in the NBA All-Star Game.
Named NBA First Team All-Star after helping the Magic compile a
57–25 record and win the Eastern Conference Atlantic Division.

1996   Named NBA First Team All-Star after the Magic compile a 60–22 record
and win the Eastern Conference Atlantic Division for the second straight year.

FIND OUT MORE

Gowdey, David. *Basketball Super Stars*. New York: Putnam, 1994.

Gutman, Bill. *Basketball*. North Bellmore, NY: Marshall Cavendish, 1990.

————. *Shaquille O'Neal: Basketball Sensation*. Brookfield, CT: Millbrook, 1994.

Hollander, Zander. *National Basketball Association Book of Fantastic Facts, Feats, and Super Stats*. Mahwah, NJ: Troll, 1995.

Weber, Bruce. *Pro Basketball Megastars*. New York: Scholastic, 1995.

How to write to Anfernee Hardaway:

Anfernee Hardaway
c/o Orlando Magic
Orlando Arena
One Magic Place
Orlando, FL 32801

INDEX